My Earth & Space Science Library

Watching the Weather

Lisa J. Amstutz

Rourke Educational Media

A Division of
Carson Dellosa Education

Before Reading: *Building Background Knowledge and Vocabulary*

Building background knowledge can help children process new information and build upon what they already know. Before reading a book, it is important to tap into what children already know about the topic. This will help them develop their vocabulary and increase their reading comprehension.

Questions and Activities to Build Background Knowledge:

1. Look at the front cover of the book and read the title. What do you think this book will be about?
2. What do you already know about this topic?
3. Take a book walk and skim the pages. Look at the table of contents, photographs, captions, and bold words. Did these text features give you any information or predictions about what you will read in this book?

Vocabulary: *Vocabulary Is Key to Reading Comprehension*

Use the following directions to prompt a conversation about each word.
- Read the vocabulary words.
- What comes to mind when you see each word?
- What do you think each word means?

> **Vocabulary Words:**
> - *forecast*
> - *hail*
> - *humid*
> - *precipitation*

During Reading: *Reading for Meaning and Understanding*

To achieve deep comprehension of a book, children are encouraged to use close reading strategies. During reading, it is important to have children stop and make connections. These connections result in deeper analysis and understanding of a book.

 Close Reading a Text

During reading, have children stop and talk about the following:
- Any confusing parts
- Any unknown words
- Text to text, text to self, text to world connections
- The main idea in each chapter or heading

Encourage children to use context clues to determine the meaning of any unknown words. These strategies will help children learn to analyze the text more thoroughly as they read.

When you are finished reading this book, turn to the last page for an **After Reading Activity**.

Table of Contents

What's the Weather?

Look outside. What do you see?

Is it raining?

Is it snowing?

Is it sunny and dry?

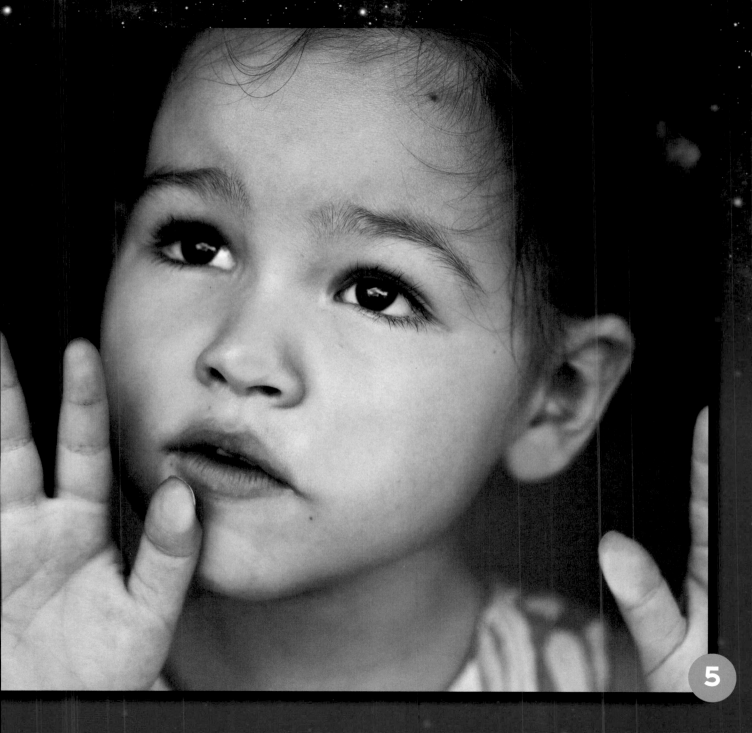

Weather is what is happening with the air outside.

Air can be hot or cold. It can be **humid** or dry. Air can be cloudy or clear.

Weather Watch

Weather changes from day to day.
A weather **forecast** tells us what
to expect.

You can see the blue sky. It will be sunny and hot today.

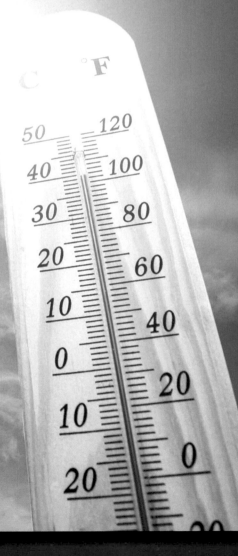

Clouds start to cover. The wind picks up speed. Rain is coming.

Drip, drop! On a warm day, rain drizzles. On a cold day, snow falls.

Hail may fall in a storm.

These are all types of **precipitation**.

15

Strong winds blow.

A hurricane dumps rain.

Take cover!

What Is Climate?

Climate is the weather in a place over many years.

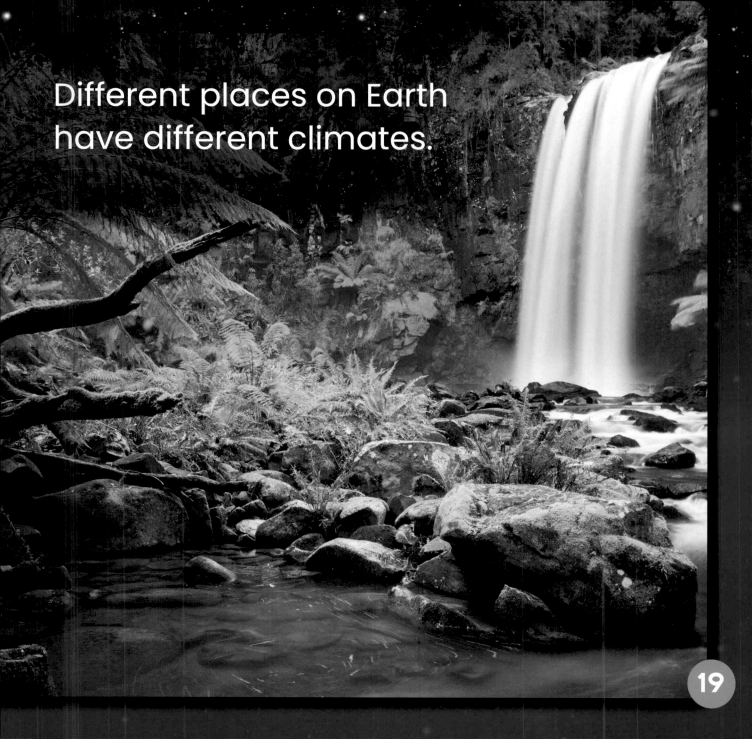

Different places on Earth have different climates.

Some places stay warm and have a lot of rain.

Some places stay cold and have very little rain.

forecast (FOR-kast): A prediction about what will happen in the future.

hail (hayl): Small balls of ice that fall from the sky.

humid (HYOO-mid): Moist and usually very warm.

precipitation (pri-sip-i-TAY-shuhn): Water falling from the sky in the form of rain, sleet, hail, or snow.

Make Your Own Rain Gauge

Want to find out how much it rains? Try making your own rain gauge!

Supplies

ruler   permanent marker

wide-mouthed glass jar

Directions

1. Use the ruler and marker to mark every quarter-inch on the outside of the jar. The numbers should start at the bottom and go up.

2. Label every half-inch with your marker.

3. Set your jar outdoors. Make sure nothing will keep rain from hitting the jar.

4. After it rains, look at the side of the jar. How much rain fell?

Index

About the Author

Lisa J. Amstutz is the author of more than 100 children's books. She loves learning about science and sharing fun facts with kids. Lisa lives on a small farm with her family, two goats, a flock of chickens, and a dog named Daisy.

After Reading Activity

Check the weather forecast for your area. Look in a newspaper or ask an adult to help you find a forecast online or on TV. What kind of weather is predicted for the next few days? Watch the weather outside each day to see if the forecast was correct.

Library of Congress PCN Data

Watching the Weather / Lisa J. Amstutz
(My Earth and Space Science Library)
ISBN (hard cover)(alk. paper) 978-1-73163-846-5
ISBN (soft cover) 978-1-73163-923-3
ISBN (e-Book) 978-1-73164-000-0
ISBN (e-Pub) 978-1-73164-077-2
Library of Congress Control Number: 2020930248

Rourke Educational Media
Printed in the United States of America
04-1062411937

Edited by: Hailey Scragg
Cover design by: Rhea Magaro-Wallace
Interior design by: Jen Bowers
Photo Credits: Cover logo: frog © Eric Phol, test tube © Sergey Lazarev, p5 © Volodina, p6 © Ig0rZh, p9 & p22 © Simonkr, p10 © yokeetod, p11 © fmajor, p12 © whiteson, p14 snow © Nastco, p14 & p22 rain © Noppharat05081977, p15 & p22 © SWInsider, p16 © deberarr, p17 © MikeMareen, p18 © cinoby, p19 & p22 sara_winter, p20 © apomares, p21 © dagsjo, All interior images from istockphoto.com.